Disclaimer

The information provided in this book is designed to provide helpful information on the subjects discussed. This book is not meant to be used, nor should it be used, to diagnose or treat any medical condition. For diagnosis or treatment of any medical problem, consult your own physician. The publisher and author are not responsible for any specific health or allergy needs that may require medical supervision and are not liable for any damages or negative consequences from any treatment, action, application, or preparation, to any person reading or following the information in this book. Any references included are provided for informational purposes only. Readers should be aware that any websites or links listed in this book may change.

Project Management

A Quick-Start Beginner's Guide For Easily Managing Projects The Right Way

By Susan Hollister

Table of Contents

Introduction

Thank you for choosing this book as your introduction to the realm of project management. By the time you finish reading, you will understand how a project is managed, from inception to completion, and will have a better idea of the roles you can play in its progress.

Project management is the process of managing a short-term venture intended to develop a unique service, product, or result. It is employed in businesses of every size and almost every industry. Many organizations, worldwide, utilize project management to stay on top of trends, to address customer service needs, and to respond to other factors that impact their profitability. Project management is so essential to the business world that there is a projected need for almost two million project managers to fill positions by the year 2025!

Just how valuable is project management? 80% of business executives around the world attribute their business success during tough economic times to project management. They view it as crucial for achieving successful objectives and staying on top of the competition. Project management has proven its effectiveness many times over. It can minimize risks and reduce costs, while improving a business's success rate. With statistics like these, project management is a must-have for any organization that wants to win.

What happens when you don't employ project management strategies? Without project planning, the organization will essentially be throwing money out the window on inefficient projects that will likely fail. Without someone to oversee a project's schedule, manage budget allocations, and coordinate the efforts of the project team, the whole project could easily become bogged down. The project's priorities could be forgotten, leading to a waste of valuable time and resources as the project runs off-course. Unforeseen risks and obstacles are more likely to ambush the project, because no one is watching out for them. A project without a project manager is unlikely to be successful; even if it does succeed, the quality of the end result will probably suffer.

Project management strategies are designed to minimize disorganization, prevent miscommunication, and prevent failure; these strategies work so successfully, it's almost like magic! Project management brings structure and order to a project, breaking it down into manageable segments that allow a team to smoothly coordinate their work and see steady progress. Project management strategies increase effective communication across the team as well as with shareholders, sponsors, and important clients.

A wise project manager makes space for each member of the team to shine. Under the project manager's guidance, a team can effectively identify potential dangers and strategize to prevent them, avoid them, or at the very least minimize their impact on the project.

Project management keeps all aspects of the project under control. It manages change, preventing project demands from becoming overwhelming. It coordinates the various parts of a project, optimizing the order in which the work is performed. The project manager sees that the necessary resources are efficiently budgeted, utilized, and accounted for. The project manager will oversee the project schedule to navigate delays and present the end results on or before the project deadline. Project management can help everything run smoothly. When hiccups do occur, the team is able to deal with them and move on swiftly, thanks to proper planning and foresight on the part of the project manager.

At the heart of project management is the manager. Project managers are unlike functional managers, individuals who are responsible for a single area of a business. Instead of being limited to a small part of the business, the project manager handles the whole ball of wax, coordinating a cross-disciplinary team in the performance of tasks that serve a single objective.

Projects are short-term in nature; the project team is drawn from multiple departments based on the needs of the project, and it operates until the project is completed. The team members then return to their various departments.

The job description for project managers varies by the project, but in general, the manager will oversee each stage of the project, from start to finish, coordinating the work of the project team, keeping the project within its original budget, and ensuring steady progress toward a timely conclusion. In short, project managers are the primary organizers of a project.

Many project managers have prior experience in management. They will have developed exceptional interpersonal communication skills and leadership qualities. The average salary range for project managers falls between $75,000 and $104,000 per year. Professional certifications are available, which reflect specific skills held by project managers.

This book contains proven steps and strategies that can help you quickly and easily learn the basics of project management or sharpen your existing management skills. This book will give you an overview of the project management process, including key strategies and the primary documents required within each part of a project.

You will learn about the four steps to a successful project, explore various management skills that can promote a successful project run, and discover other factors that help drive a project to completion.

Next, you will get an in-depth look at the planning stage, possibly the most important part of a project, because it lays out the guidelines and boundaries that will guide the direction of the project. You'll learn to write a scope statement, use proven strategies for estimating resources. You'll find instructions for creating a financial plan and budget, quality plans, communication guidelines, and risk management plans. You'll learn about procurement strategies and how to set up for acceptance testing.

In Chapter 3, you will explore even more strategies that can make a project run efficiently and effectively.

We will review and affirm the qualities that make a project manager great. You will be able to identify areas of strength in your own life that will help you immensely in your career. This includes time management strategies the best project managers utilize to help complete projects on time. Unlike basic time management skills, which most managers have mastered, there are some skills specific to project management; I will familiarize you with the basics of each.

Finally, you will discover how to end a project, how to effectively conduct closing activities and ensure that nothing is left unresolved. It is important to finish well. The information I have provided will equip you to finish your projects in a way that provides comprehensive closure to all the parties involved.

We begin by discussing what defines a project, and summarizing in brief how one goes about managing it.

Chapter 1: Project Management, An Introduction

What is a project? What is project management? According to the dictionary, a **project** is, "something that is contemplated, devised, or planned," or a "plan; scheme." In business, a project is different from an organization's day-to-day operations. Operations are usually repetitive, tried and true systems an organization uses on a regular basis. A **program**, on the other hand is a group of projects that are managed together because they are related.

While operations and programs usually become permanent fixtures within a company, projects are short-term and temporary; they exist to find a creative solution to a specific problem. Project solutions may result in the creation of a new product or the development of a special service.

A project comes into play when the organization lacks a systematic approach for handling a specific problem. This new approach probably will never be reused in the future, making it a one-time event, therefore a project. You can often distinguish a project from a regular operation or a program by looking for the following characteristics of a project:

- A project has a limited scope.

- A project may be required to follow risky means develop a solution.

- A project may require specific tools, technology, expertise or resources beyond what the organization already possesses.

- Projects may require a unique location. For example, a research project may need to take place out in the field rather than in your offices.

- A project carries a limited time frame; it is not ongoing.

- A project has the distinguishing feature of **progressive elaboration**. Progressive elaboration is the practice of revealing and narrowing down the details of the work as the project moves forward.

Why Project Management?

A few organizations view project management as unnecessary and a needless expense. The most successful businesses, however, are firmly convinced; they've experienced the benefits – and the consequences of living without project management – themselves.

Project management is defined as "the process of planning, organizing, staffing, directing, and controlling the production of a system." It is a widespread strategy that businesses of all shapes and sizes can utilize. It often relies on a team of employees each with their own skills and expertise, to move a project from a beginning phase to its completion. These teams are important because they enable the business owners and executives to focus on what they do best – overseeing and managing the businesses – while the teams focus on bringing their skills together to create a useful solution for a problem beyond the scope of business management.

Project managers often have seasoned backgrounds in other areas of management such as risk management or contingency planning. Project management relies on multiple employees bringing together skills from all sorts of backgrounds to create the best solution possible. The various activities performed within the team create a chain of events that ultimately lead to the final outcome. For example, one team member may be great at planning and can fuel the planning stage of the project, while another team member brings his cost and risk management skills to the table to design an efficient budget. Another member will use her time-management skills to ensure that milestones are reached and the project is completed on time.

Project management is useful for several reasons. Project managers can often double the organization's return on investment by minimizing the use of resources through the maximizing of efficiencies. The output of a project can often help the organization minimize its expenses while increasing its employee productivity. Project management often requires a great deal of creativity and innovation, which is something other employees working within the organization's usual constraints may not be able to provide.

Finally, and most importantly, the field of project management has developed a body of best practices that have been proven effective over decades of use. The basic process, around which all the other practices are built is a four-stage system. This system enables a team to lay out a project from beginning to end, prioritize and sequentially order the component parts, minimize the larger risks, overcome various roadblocks, and coordinate their work to ultimately deliver a finished product on time and within budget.

The Four Stages of Project Management

Project Plan

Project Management Stages

The **initiation, planning, executing** and **closing** stages must each be completed in their turn before moving on to the next phase. Each stage is described below.

The Initiation Phase

The initiation phase marks the beginning of a new project. During this stage, the organization identifies the objectives, scope, purpose and deliverables to be produced. It then obtains the authorization to do the actual work. The organization assigns a project manager, allocates an initial amount of money toward the project, and identifies the various project stakeholders. The primary outcomes of this stage are three documents, the project charter, the stakeholder register, and the project review form.

The **project charter** includes a project justification, goals for the project, the clear definition of the project's scope, anticipated risks and roadblocks, and each of the project's most critical delivery points. It includes the names of customers and corporate collaborators, also known as the **stakeholder register**. The project charter also defines the roles and tasks of each team member and gives a summary of the general direction to take in order to reach a solution.

Next, the organization will create a **project manager job description**. The description should contain information that describes the function of the project manager as well as the qualifications and experience an applicant will need. The objective of a superior project manager is to achieve the project objectives successfully by balancing time, cost, quality, and scope. The job description should describe the organization's expectations for the role and list the salary and information about the **project management office.**

The final step of the initiation phase is to complete a **project review form**. The project review form allows the project manager to efficiently communicate with the project's sponsors, who will want regular updates on its progress. Project reviews are generally produced at the end of a project stage.

For the initiation stage, the project review form will include updates regarding whether or not the project is scheduled to be completed on time, whether the organization has enough money set aside for the project, and whether there are any unresolved roadblocks at this point. It should also include information on how the organization has handled any uncovered risks and whether the project's output so far has been approved. The main purpose of the project review form is to gain approval from its sponsor to move on to the next stage.

The Planning Phase

The planning phase is where the project manager and team begin to develop the path to the output in more detail. The main purpose of this stage is to lay out a plan of action. The **plan** is a written document that contains all of the information that will allow the project to move forward. Like a business plan, it is a living and breathing document that will be modified as needed while the project progresses.

It is simple to think of the plan as a roadmap. It should define the scope of the project and list all milestones to mark its progress toward completion. It should also include information on each phase of the project and the various tasks the team will work on throughout its lifespan. The plan will show which team members are in charge of which tasks, and establish tentative due dates for each task.

Most importantly, the plan should include an in-depth schedule that will lay the project out from start to finish. The plan may only start out as a couple of paragraphs at the beginning of the planning phase but it should grow into a more complex plan toward the end of this stage, as the information starts to come together. It is the project manager's job to review the plan daily and compare it to the team's actual status.

The main plan will include several sub-plans that apply to specific aspects of the project:

- The **resource plan** is a document containing important information about all of the resources the team will need, ranging from labor costs to tools, to make the project successful. One of the most important aspects of a resource plan is a **resource schedule.** This schedule allows the team to plan out how much of each resource they will need, and for what parts of the project. This allows the team to share resources, often saving costs. The resource plan lists the types of labor the project needs, the number of roles to be filled, and the responsibilities of each role. It should also list the quantity of equipment and other materials the project will need in order to move ahead.

- The **financial plan** uses the resource plan to detail the amount of money each resource will require. It includes a detailing of costs associated with administration and contingency planning, while listing each expense. The main purpose of the financial plan is to provide a basis for comparison between the project's overall budget and its actual total cost.

- The **quality plan** allows the team to measure the quality of specific achievements within the project and to ensure the output meets their qualitative expectations. The project manager can use the quality plan to set deadlines for quality control and assurance activities to ensure the project stays on track and that the right team members are working on the right tasks. The quality plan will set out the criteria by which the output is measured. It will also set the acceptable limits for the project output.

- The **risk plan** takes an in-depth look at all the risks, potential roadblocks, and other issues that may arise in the course of the project and explores ways to minimize possible negative impacts. It can increase a team's chances of achieving successful outcomes, simply by raising awareness of possible problems and setting strategies in place ahead of time to deal with them.

A risk plan lays out every risk associated with the project and organizes them by category and then by priority. It can assist the team in determining which risks are most likely to occur, allowing the members to spend their time more efficiently. This plan also lays out the impact each risk may have on the project if not minimized.

The project management team uses the risk plan to develop and implement preventative measures, map out contingency plans, and track each risk throughout the life of the project. A risk plan is an essential step in the planning process, since it can dramatically decrease the likelihood of mishaps seriously undermining the project.

- The **acceptance plan** serves as the bridge between the project's output and its ultimate users. This plan will oversee development of the end product so that it will be acceptable to customers. After all, it's the users' formal acceptance that will mark the project a success. An acceptance plan will review the details of all project outputs and define the standards required for customer acceptance. Teams can use this plan to determine how they will test the output and to help them identify any resources they may need for testing purposes.

- The purpose of a **communications plan** is to help the team communicate key information to the right people at the right time and in the right way. The communication plan should include detailed information about the project as a whole with all of its goals, deadlines, strategies, and tasks clearly laid out. The plan should specifically identify all shareholders and their individual communication requirements while listing an anticipated schedule of communications activities. In the process, the team can use the communication plan to gather feedback on their methods of communication.

- The **procurement plan** establishes how the team will obtain resources from outside suppliers. An ideal procurement plan will identify, quantify, and list each needed resource. It should also describe when and how money will be allocated to obtain those resources. Teams can use the procurement plan to examine what tasks will be necessary and how to procure resources efficiently.

The Tender Process

Once the procurement plan is complete, the next step is to begin the process of connecting with suppliers. Project management teams usually refer to this as the **tender process**. The tender process includes the development of several documents that will help the team manage procurement and pick the best suppliers available:

- The **statement of work** defines and clarifies the type of work the team needs from a supplier. It will generally include details such as the supplier type, the resources the team needs, a schedule of due dates and a copy of payment terms and conditions.

- Next is the **request for information (RFI)** document. This document helps the team identify the needs of the supplier while building a bridge of communication with potential vendors. This document is well known across multiple industries and is the accepted way to solicit external suppliers.

- Subsequent to the request for information document is the **request for proposal (RFP)**, which can help the team choose the best supplier by communicating the team's needs in detail, so that the potential vendors can submit a firm proposal.

- Next is the **supplier contract**, which is essentially the document that lays out the terms and conditions between the organization and the supplier. The contract should specifically note all resources the supplier will deliver, all due dates and invoicing information. It should also lay out the terms and conditions for both parties. This document will be signed by both parties as a binding contract.

- Finally, the team will need **tender forms** to track everything that occurs throughout the process of selecting vendors.

The final step of the planning stage is another **project review**. At this point in the process, the project review form should denote whether the project is scheduled to be completed on time, whether it has met the budget to date and whether any existing roadblocks and risks have been cleared. It should also list any resources and materials that have been accepted during the planning process.

The Execution Phase

The execution phase is the most hands-on and often the most exciting part of a project. In this stage, the team starts work on developing the final project output. This is the largest and most time-consuming stage of the project, as it's where all the planning gets implemented in full force. Due to the complex nature of this project phase, certain management strategies are used to help track and manage the multiple factors that are running simultaneously.

Although this stage may sound grueling, the good news is that these management strategies simplify the entire process. Once they're learned, they can easily carry over into many aspects of your life, both personal and professional, making things run much more smoothly and effectively.

Nine management strategies appear front and center during this phase of the project:

- **Time management** is the process of overseeing and regulating how much time one spends on a task. In the case of a project, time management becomes the process of managing how much time each team member spends on tasks that are relevant to the project. The greatest benefit of implementing a time management strategy is to help teams ensure that they can deliver the output on time and use their time wisely, focusing on the most important tasks first and putting less important tasks off to the side when possible. As you have discovered so far, there are many schedules involved in the initiating and planning process, so using superior time management skills can positively impact a project's end result.

- **Cost management** is the process of managing all expenses related to the project. The best way to track expenses it to have a set of **expense forms** that allows each team member to record expenses for different parts of the project. Expense forms also make it easier for the project manager to review and authenticate large purchases. The cost management process allows teams to define individual costs related to the project and can serve as an excellent record-keeping system. A cost management strategy can help the team ensure the project stays within budget and that all invoices are paid in a timely manner. It can also help the team avoid overspending.

- **Quality management**, as you may have guessed, is the process of managing and improving the quality of the final output. The quality management process can assist the team in setting measurable target quality goals and identify potential risks and roadblocks that may lead to poor quality if unaddressed. It's also a great way to monitor the progress of quality assurance. One helpful strategy is to utilize **quality review forms** to measure whether quality goals and standards are being met and whether any changes are needed for improvement.

- **Change management** is the strategy put in place to help project managers track and control all of the change requests within the project. Change requests can become overwhelming without proper organization and management. Implementing change management can help the team pay attention to change requests and measure the practicability of each one. This management strategy can also help the team keep track of all changes that were approved as opposed to those that were denied. Without proper change management strategies, the scope of a project can easily veer off course, causing a negative impact on the outcome of the project.

- **Risk management** is the process of watching and regulating all risks associated with the project. The risk management process helps the team differentiate between the most vital risks and those that are less important, allowing it to prioritize responses with ease. Each risk is analyzed in detail and ranked in importance from most to least critical. This process makes it easier for the team as a whole to determine which risks need the most attention first.

- **Issue management** is similar to risk management in that it is another process for preventing failure within a project. However, it focuses on roadblocks from outside sources, rather than internal risks that threaten project completion. For example, issue management can help the team in the event that a labor problem arises or when a supplier may not be able to fulfill the team's requests. The issue management process allows the team to lay out each issue and analyze each one in detail. The team can then rank all issues in order from most critical to least so that they can make the most efficient decisions. A proper issue management process can enable the team to quickly identify and develop solutions.

- **Procurement management** is the process of developing and managing a solid purchasing strategy. This process can enable the team to develop piece by piece instructions on how to determine which resources and services they need, how to choose a supplier, how to put in an order to each supplier, how to schedule deliveries efficiently, how to receive the deliveries and how to accept payments from the supplier.

- **Acceptance management** is the process of ensuring that the output will meet the needs set by the customers. Acceptance management generally implements **user acceptance testing** to ensure the output's standards. The testing process allows real customers to review the product and determine whether or not it is ready for the masses. Acceptance management also makes it easy to organize the testing results.

- **Communications management** is the process of determining how to keep up communications between the team and its most important players by only emitting the most important information at the most efficient times. By implementing a communications management strategy, the project manager will know what key information must be collected and who needs to be a part of the communication process. This strategy will assist the team in deciding how and when the information will be delivered as well as which communication media are most important for getting that specific information across. Communications management also grants the team the time to develop and review its messages before they are sent out. Regular communication reviews will also help improve the team's communication accuracy as the project progresses.

The final part of the execution stage is the project review. Again, the project review form will contain how the project is progressing toward completion, if it is under-budget to date, and what roadblocks or risks have been cleared during this stage. It should specifically note if any outputs were formally accepted during this stage.

The Closing Phase

We've now reached the final stage of the project management process. This phase allows the team to officially close down the project and deliver all up current information to the project sponsors. In this stage, the team will deliver the output to its customers, transfer all documentation created throughout the process to be archived, close out relationships with suppliers, disband the team, returning members to their original organizations, and return any borrowed equipment.

A final project review marks the official end of this stage. Its purpose is to determine whether the project was a failure or a success and to identify any potential lessons that may have been learned through the process. Even though the team has already released the output to its customers, it is still important for the team to complete this project review together. Psychologically, it provides a sense of closure and practically, it allows the members to communicate what they've learned to the team as a whole.

The first responsibility at this stage is to compile a **project closure report**. This report will lay out all the principles required for the project's completion, identify any project-related issues that may remain unresolved, and present the delivery of – and if necessary, a maintenance plan for – the end-product. It should also contain a plan for transferring all relevant documentation to the parent organization. This includes copies of cancelled supplier contracts, items documenting the return of all other resources to third-party businesses and formally denoting the project's closure.

The second responsibility is the **post project review**. This review enables the team to point out any significant successes within the project, present the outputs and review all milestones and learned lessons.

From what we've described so far, it looks like a stage's primary activity is limited to that stage. This is mostly true. When one stage ends, the next one opens up. However, it is critically important to ensure continuity from one stage to the next. This idea reinforces the concept of progressive elaboration; the details developed in one stage are carried through into the next, influencing how the project unfolds in all subsequent stages.

For example, although planning seems limited to the first stage, the planning process will continue throughout all four stages. Some items will be repeated in more than one stage, but when it reappears, it will serve a purpose unique to that stage.

What Makes a Project Successful?

Throughout this chapter, you may have noticed the phrases, "to make the project successful," or "successful project," or "achieve success", but we haven't spent much time talking about what the word "success" means in the context of project management. While a project's success is broadly defined as "to deliver a quality and customer-approved output", there is much more to it than that.

The terms "quality" and "customer approval" are further defined by three factors a team must always balance out: **cost, time,** and **scope**. A team cannot necessarily predict the cost and time needed for a project but they do have control over the scope of the project. Scope sets the project's boundaries. It defines what the team is responsible for and – of equal importance – what it is *not* responsible for. Only after the scope is established, can objectives and goals be clearly defined.

Scope is usually defined during the first stage. The most important purpose of the scope is that it sets the project's limitations.

The team must manage the scope, with the help of the project manager, so that it correctly and efficiently fits the size of the project. Anything outside of the scope's proper range can have negative effects on the outcome of the project.

Changes in scope during mid-project are known as **scope creep**. When scope creep occurs, it can cause harmful changes by introducing new risks such as higher costs, budget problems, a lower return on investment, or staffing problems. Proper change management strategies can often minimize scope creep and mitigate any effects that may occur.

Without Project Management: A Cautionary Tale

Let's take a look at what happens when a team does not have a project manager to set the scope of its project, nor to utilize proper change management procedures:

One year, two electronic data system organizations paired up to create a national gun registration system for Canada. The project was originally supposed to be a small one that would cost the citizens of Canada $2 million. However, since gun control is a major political issue, many interest groups got involved and began influencing the project until at least 1,000 change requests were made within the first couple of years of the project. As a result, work the team did not originally plan or budget for occurred; this ended up costing the citizens of Canada $688 million with $75 million per year accumulating in maintenance costs. The project would end up costing $1 billion by 2004, but would not generate enough revenue to make it a worthwhile investment. Had the project set forth limitations to their scope and exercised more effective change management, this project may have been successful.

Project management provides processes that help organizations produce successful results every day. Research shows that 70% of organizations who hire project managers report dramatic increases in the success rate of their projects. Let's take a look at the process of project planning.

Chapter 2: The Project Planning Process

As you may have inferred from the previous chapter, the planning stage is one of the most critical stages in the project management process. This is where the roadmap for a project is defined and laid down to establish a pathway toward the successful provision of the project's output. In this chapter, we will explore planning in greater depth. After completing this chapter, you should be able to confidently and knowledgably conduct the planning phase of your next project.

The first thing you should do in this stage is choose a **project name**. It may seem irrelevant but the name of a project can make a huge difference in guiding the project forward. It's easy to just refer to a project as "Marketing Project" or "Sales Project" but those titles do not give much indication as to what the project is actually about. A couple better examples would be "Develop a Marketing Strategy to Boost Chicken Sandwich Sales in New York," or "Create a Sales Strategy to Acquire New Target Audience." These are much more appealing, more detailed, and can better help guide the direction of the project.

Defining Scope

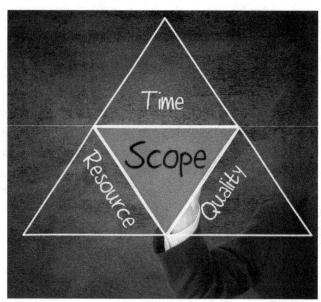
Project Scope

Creating a **scope statement** is the second step of the planning process. As you learned from the case study in Chapter 1, failing to define the scope of the project indicates poor change management, which can easily lead to project failure. A scope statement is a written document that details multiple factors regarding the project, including the basis for the project, the standards required for the output of the project, objectives, exclusions, limitations, and forecasts.

The scope statement defines the boundaries of a project, clearly describing what is – and more importantly – what is *not* part of the project. It serves as a **binding contract** between the organization, its shareholders, team members, and others involved in the project. Their signatures are required as their commitment to their part in the project.

It is understood that this statement is a best guess, given the current level of information available, and that adjustments to the statement may well be necessary as the project develops. Those changes can be requested at any stage of the project in the form of change request documentation and are signed off by the stakeholders.

Here is the key information you will want to gather before you begin to build your scope statement:

- **Basis** – Give a concise description of the project's purpose. In other words, why is the project imperative to the organization? Remember to keep this statement brief; the project charter will provide a more detailed description.

- **Output Scope** – Describe the project's desired output and what, specifically is included.

- **Acceptance Standards** – Provide a set of acceptance standards that dictate the criteria the team must meet before the final output can be considered complete.

- **Project Outputs** – Describe specifically what the project will deliver.

- **Project Exclusions** – Describe what will *not* be achieved or delivered by the project.

- **Project Limitations** – List anything that might stand in a way of what the project can achieve. Include strategies that will allow the team to navigate around those limitations and describe the costs that will be incurred in the process.

Project Foresight – The planning process involves putting together what you already know and assumptions you used when making your estimations. Include strategies that will serve to guide the team through project challenges.

The Project Scope Statement

Now that you know exactly what to include in your scope statement, you're ready to begin creating it. Let's break it down into easy, manageable step-by-step instructions:

- Start a new document. Write the name of your organization at the center of the first page.

- Your **table of contents** will go on the second page. This will be populated as you write; you'll come back to update it when you're finished writing.

- The next piece will be an **executive summary** derived from the project charter. This summary should include a clear and concise, yet specific summary of what the project is about and why it is necessary.

- The **business objectives** section follows. Here you will detail why the project will benefit the organization. You can include how the need was first recognized. You will want to list any factors that contributed to the need, such as staff layoffs or budget cuts. Include predictions of what may happen to the organization and its customers if the need is not met. At the same time, you'll want to enumerate the benefits you expect to be realized due to the results of this project. Then you should list any alternative solutions that have been considered, and explain why this particular solution was chosen in the end.

- A **description of the chosen solution** should follow the business objectives section. This section will relay how the product, service or result will meet a specific business need. Include how it will benefit the organization. Detail the standards the final solution must meet in order to deem the project a success. You will end this section with a detailed description of the final deliverable.

- The next section should be about the **project description** itself. This section should include details about the project's scope, summarizing your scope statement from above. You will include how the team intends to measure success and indicate whether this project is dependent upon the successful completion of any other separate projects.

- You will follow this with a table that describes the **roles and functions** of the project sponsor, project owner, project manager, shareholders, and members of the project team. Any known vendors or outside subject matter experts that will be used, should be identified here.

- The next section provides a detailed description of how the team plans to approach the work. This description should include any **plans** to break the project into manageable stages and an explanation of any intentions to outsource, how the team intends to test the final solution, and any additional practical considerations that play into the process.

- The next section will contain an **estimated schedule** of events regarding the project. It should indicate the starting date of the project, the proposed end date, and major milestones along the way. An estimated schedule of resources should follow the main schedule of events and identify the types of resources called for, as well as what they will be used for and how long they will be needed.

- Following the estimated resource schedule will be an **estimated budget schedule** that details when and how money is planned to be spent throughout the course of the project, along with a financial forecast.

- A **project control** section will follow the various schedules. This is the section where the team can fill in future information regarding meetings, status reports, and different sub-sets of management: change, issue, risk, and communication.

- The final section of the scope statement will be an **authorization page** that names the people responsible for contributing to the project; these individuals will have the authority to approve changes to the statement, adjustments to the project in its entirety, and responsibility to approve the final solutions.

- You will conclude the document with space for the signatures of everyone associated with the project.

Planning Resources

Once your team has developed the scope statement, they can then move on to creating the **activity resource plan**. Activity resource planning is the process of determining what resources are needed to successfully complete the various activities and how and when those resources will be obtained and used. A solid resource plan includes the details of every type of resource needed for the project and will detail the various resources – including individual team members – necessary to complete each activity.

The most common resource categories are:

- People

- Knowledge

- Money

- Physical equipment

- Time

- Materials

In the beginning of a project, little is known about these details, but they will become more clearly defined as you begin to look into what needs to be accomplished to reach the end result. As individual activities are separated out, you will be able to organize them into sequential groupings.

In any project, there will be tasks that can be accomplished independently and steps that must be completed before other steps can begin. Instead of stringing them together in a single sequence, it saves time to create multiple sequences that can be run more-or-less simultaneously. When drawn up effectively, the resources will be shared efficiently across the various tasks, minimizing the "down time" for any particular resource. You optimize resource sharing by developing a **project network.**

The Network Diagram

This network is represented by a **network diagram**, a series of nodes, which represent individual activities, linked by lines indicating their relationships to other activities. This visual representation makes it easy to see how the component parts of the project fit together. The first network diagrams were drawn by hand, but today there are numerous software products that can assist you in defining tasks and in designing the optimal network.

Once you have figured out the type and quantity of resources you'll need, the time it will take to obtain and utilize them, and who will be in charge of what, you can lay everything out in a **resource schedule.** While this can be written up by hand, I recommend using one of the many software packages that are available for this purpose. They save time and have built-in safeguards to prevent you from double-booking any one resource. You must also ensure that all of the resources you will be readily available before you sign off on the schedule, which will also be approved by the other stakeholders.

One of the variables to consider when building your network diagram is when different resources will be available. For example, if a certain subject matter expert will be available only during the first week of June, you'll need to arrange your tasks so that whatever you need that expert for will fall within that time frame. If a piece of rented equipment is used in four different tasks, you'll want to schedule those four tasks, regardless of the strands of the network on which they reside, in such a way that the equipment can be shared among them with minimal down time.

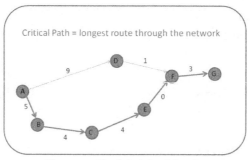

How to Find Critical Path

Once your network diagram is drawn up, you be able to determine its all-important **critical path.** A critical path is the longest sequence of events, from start to end of the project, which cannot be shortened. If an activity on this chain of activities is not completed by its scheduled deadline, it will delay the completion of the entire project.

An activity known as **estimating the resources** is usually one of the first activities in designing the resource plan. It is important to refer to the scope statement and any information conceived during the initiation phase to identify any activities and/or milestones that will require necessary resources. Here are a few techniques you can use to help get the process started:

- **Bring in an Expert** - In this technique, the project manager consults with an expert who has previously done work in the field that is related to the project. An expert can usually give great advice on where to start in terms of resources.

- **Analyze Alternatives** – In this technique, the project manager and team brainstorm different ways that they can assign resources to the project. This often involves putting together possible scenarios using different types and different quantities of resources until you find the combination that makes most sense.

- **Published Data** – In this technique, the project manager turns to scholarly articles and other publications that report on similar projects from other organizations.

- **Bottom Up Estimation** – In this technique, the team breaks the project down into separate activities where they estimate the resources for each part and then put everything together for a complete estimate. While this technique is the most accurate of them all, it can be extremely time consuming and costly.

Resource Estimation

Once you've done the work to determine the different activities and their resources your project includes, you'll be able to estimate the time it takes to complete them. Task estimates are measured in hours, days, weeks and months; tasks will be fit into a schedule to minimize overlaps and limitations. The duration estimation must take into account the activity itself, its scope, and the availability of needed resources. Smaller activities are often measured in hours or days while large-scale activities may take weeks or months to complete.

It is also important to balance time with how you divide the labor; the more team members you assign to work on a large-scale task, the less time it may require. Another thing you'll want to take into consideration is the cost of each resource, as you will need that information for the next step in planning.

Your team members will agree on a rough estimate, derived from information they have at hand. To refine this estimate, here are some strategies you may choose to employ:

- **Bring in an Expert** – This technique calls upon experts to offer their advice on how long they think each activity will take. Your experts may well come from within the team itself. Many team members will have likely worked on other projects before and can offer invaluable wisdom when estimating necessary labor, other resources, and cost or time requirements.

- **Mirror Estimation** – Here you compare your project to a similar successful project. You will base your estimations on how long it took in the earlier project. For this technique to be effective, the two projects must be very similar.

- **Software Estimation** – This technique involves taking data from previous projects and plugging it into a software formula to calculate the estimated times of completion for various activities.

- **Trio Estimation** – In this technique, the team comes up with a realistic duration, a best-case duration and a worst-case estimate for each activity. The average of all three numbers is selected as the actual estimation.

Financial Planning

Once the resource planning is complete, the next step is to focus on the financial planning. The **financial plan** enables you to compare the sum cost of each resource and other project expenses against with the project's budget. This plan can help you cut back, shuffle funds where most needed, and create a little cushion for unexpected events. You can create a financial plan by hand or use the help of project management software.

There are two types of financial plans: **top-down** and **bottom-up**. A top-down plan is one where you already know your total budget and you allocate funds until you have reached the limit. A bottom-up plan is one where you don't know how much the project will cost until you add up each expense.

There is no right or wrong way to figure out your financial plan. It usually depends on the way your project is structured and what you know about the funds that will be used. The top-down plan makes it easy to stay within budget, since the line has already been drawn in the sand. The bottom-up plan gives you pinpoint accuracy, to the extent that *anything* can be predicted in project management; it gives you more creativity in choosing resources and the opportunity to appeal for the funds you actually need.

Determine Core Costs

Before you actually create the plan, it is important to determine which expenses are your **core costs** and which are **non-core costs**. Core costs are expenses that are necessary in order to produce a successful output. Things like equipment and labor fall under this category. Non-core costs are anything outside of the absolute essentials that the project may still require, such as insurance, legal counsel, travel expenses, etc.

Once you have identified or estimated the costs of these expenses, it is a good idea to see how much money is left over, in case some of the estimates are wrong or a hidden expense pops up at some point. It's always helpful to have a little extra money to fall back on in the case of a snag. Even if you're only able to estimate the costs at this point, it's a good idea to set aside 10% of your funds for contingencies.

When all your numbers have been calculated, you can represent them in a visual plan. The simplest way to create a visual financial plan for your project by hand is to use the spreadsheet option that comes with your word processor. Keep in mind, however, that most project management software will provide a core cost calculator.

You will break down your project by discrete stages and budget within those stages. Under each project stage, you can cost out individual tasks that need to be accomplished in order to complete that stage.

Next to each task, you'll list the labor costs, labor hours, material costs, and any other resource costs that will be incurred by the task. At the bottom of each category, a subtotal line will show the total cost for that activity. You can then use those calculations to come up with a total cost for the project. You compare this to your budget and tweak the numbers as needed to see where savings can be found, given different scheduling and resourcing options.

Quality Plan

The next step in the planning process is to create the **quality plan**. The quality plan is a document that outlines the tasks that will produce an output that meets or exceeds the customers' standards. The purpose of a quality plan is to provide the team and shareholders with easy and organized access to quality standards of the project. A quality plan typically lays out the quality standards necessary to satisfy the customer and lists how the team can achieve them. Teams can often achieve quality standards by utilizing events such as peer reviews, checklists, plans, etc. or by using quality resources. A quality plan can also help the team to measure quality throughout the duration of the project.

A proper quality plan should roughly contain 11 elements:

- **A Purpose Statement** – This statement should be at the beginning of the document and describe the purpose of the quality plan. This section is an opportunity to describe briefly any policies, standards and procedures that the team will elaborate on in the rest of the plan.

- **Management Roles** – The next section should identify the roles and responsibility of all team members. You can easily organize this in a table that lists the name of the team member, their role within the project overall and their responsibility in terms of quality assurance. For example, Joe Smith, the project manager, may be responsible for performing quality audits throughout the project. Underneath this table, you can include a table that lists any tools or resources that the team will use measure quality.

- **Existing QM Systems** – This section should define any existing quality management systems within the organization. Many organizations will already have quality planning, quality assurance and quality control systems in place but it will vary from organization to organization. The purpose of this section is to identify any existing standards that relate to the current project and determine how to use them to achieve quality. The team will often look for things such as federal regulations, customer goals, success factors and helpful data. Teams can often use this opportunity to identify and eliminate gaps in quality. This is also where the team can brainstorm ways to improve quality, attain it quicker and/or achieve it for much less.

- **Design Control** – This section should outline the details of design control if the final output is going to be a physical product. This section can contain design reviews, document changes in design and include any necessary sign-offs.

- **Document Control** – This section should outline the plan on how to keep all documents related to the project organized during each stage. Nothing is a worse set up for failure than missing or unorganized documents.

- **Procurement Strategies** – Here, the team can outline and identify any standards that must come from purchasing anything needed to move the project forward. It is important for the project manager and team to determine all the resources they will need to procure, and establish selection standards for potential vendors.

  This section should explore building strong supplier relationships as well as drafting quality contracts that will ensure the timely delivery of all resources as well as lay out the terms of the agreement. It can also identify the procedures that the team will use to review and approve all resources. Procurement quality control can include scheduling regular meetings with suppliers, delivery tracking and contract changes.

- **Testing Information** – This section should provide details on acceptance and integration testing on the final output.

- **Corrections** – This section should contain information on what the team will do in the event that any problems come up during execution.

- **Records of Quality** – This section contains information on how the team and the organization will maintain quality assurance records during and after the project is complete.

- **Audits** – This section should contain information on how internal audits will be planned and implemented for each stage of the project.

- **Training Guidelines** – This section should identify any areas of training that will be necessary for any team members.

- It is important to remember that the quality of the quality plan is equally important because without specific and accurate details, the overall quality of the project can decrease.

Managing Risk

Following the quality plan is the **risk management plan**. Creating a risk management plan during the planning stage is extremely important for minimizing risks and reducing the chances of a small snag turning into a huge contingency. The main objective of this plan is to identify the chances of a potential problem happening and then assessing how those problems could impact the project. There are many different kinds of risks – cost-related risks, non-cost-related risks, physical risk and legal risks to name a few. There are also several methods to reduce risk, which includes eliminating the risk all together or trying to balance out the risk to lessen its impact on the project. Sometimes the team will actually accept the risk but that will often happen following a cost-benefit analysis. Often times, the team will prioritize each risk during the planning stage to see which ones are worth working to reduce/eliminate versus which ones may not be worth spending time on. There are generally five steps in drafting the risk management plan.

Identify Each Risk. Begin by listing every potential risk, including even the smallest of possible outcomes. You can do this by brainstorming a few simple questions:

- What *could* happen?

- How *likely* is it to happen?

- How *severe* can the impact be?

- How can we *reduce* the chances of it happening? By how much?

- How can we *lessen* the impact if it does happen? By how much?

It is easier and helpful to break each part of the project into smaller, separate topics and analyze each one for risks. You could break the project into topics such as cost, legalities, liabilities, etc. I would also recommend looking into similar, previously completed projects and see what kind of risks were found to give you some ideas and to ensure that you've exhausted all options

Prioritize Each Risk. Once you have compiled a list of potential risks, the next step is to prioritize them based on level of impact and chances of it happening. The more severe the impact and the more likely it is to happen, the higher it should be on the list. Measure every risk until you have ranked each one. The equation for calculating risk is: Risk = probability **x** impact.

Plan For Each Risk– After prioritizing each risk, the next step is to develop an action plan for each one in the event that it actually occurs. The risks at the top of the list are likely to have more in-depth action plans than those near the bottom. The action plans should answer questions such as:

- Who will be responsible?

- How will they respond?

- What is the contingency plan?

- Since every project is different, the answers for each plan will be unique.

Assign Human Resources. Now that you have developed an action plan for each risk, the next step is to assign team members to certain roles within each plan so that everyone is ready and prepared in the event of a risk occurring. You can also select team members to track each risk and look for cues that may be able to signify whether the probability of a risk is changing from high to low or vice versa.

Communicate the Plan. After everything is completed, the final step is to communicate the risk management plan to all shareholders and anyone else outside of the team who is involved with the project. Ensure that they are all aware of the contingency plans, and who is in charge of dealing with an actual occurrence.

The Acceptance Plan

Once the risk management plan has been completed, the next step is to move on to developing the **acceptance plan**. Acceptance planning is a critical point in the project because it serves as the bridge between the output and the customers. The acceptance plan will help the customers "accept" the output, therefore making the project a success.

Create Your Acceptance Plan Template

At this point in the planning stage, it is important to develop an acceptance planning template that can later be filled in with the help of the team and the customer during the actual acceptance process. You can draw up an acceptance plan template using these steps:

- Create a cover page with the name of your organization and the name of the project.

- Reserve the next page for your table of contents; you will update this when you are finished.

- The **first** chapter of the document will be the **Overview.** Section 1.1 will be the **Purpose**; in it, you describe the user acceptance strategy and state all requirements as set forth in the rest of the plan. The purpose is also used to communicate the progress of the project to the shareholders. The purpose should also note any other audience targets.

- Next is Section 1.2, the **Scope**, which briefly describes the scope of the acceptance plan, noting factors that will be tested and whether for the scope encompasses a single project or a set of projects. Section 1.3 will describe the **Output** to be delivered after acceptance testing along with the results. It describes the way the results will be measured and any recommendations as a result of the testing. Section 1.4 will include a list of shareholders and their association with the acceptance testing to conclude the overview section.

- The **second** chapter will contain all of the information on **Testing**. Section 2.1 will summarize the **General Approach,** which should include an overview of how the output will be tested. This information usually consists of naming the testing venue, discussing how the testing will be carried out, how many times the output will be tested, and any other important details. An acceptance plan should note if an output is going to be tested in cycles, which means each cycle will focus on correcting any problems found in the previous cycle

- Section 2.2 is the **Unit Testing** section. If your project is small then you can skip this section. Unit testing is helpful for large projects that can be broken down into smaller individual components. This section will list who is testing what and leave room to describe the testing standards, procedures, and test results. Both functional and specification testing may be performed in this setting to compare the output against the design and to look for any systematic errors.

- Section 2.3 will be the actual **Acceptance Testing** module where the output is tested as a whole, as if it were already available to the public. This section will list which business units are responsible for the acceptance testing and who will be managing it. This section should include a list of testing standards, including specific tests such as security and/or safety.

- The **third** chapter is the **Responsibilities** section, which lists the acceptance testing manager, the testing team and their respective roles and responsibilities. The general responsibilities of the acceptance testing manager are to develop the acceptance testing plan and testing standards, oversee the training of the testing team, gather the testing data, oversee any changes or modifications to the testing methods, and monitor the progress of the testing schedule. The testing team will consist of several people and their responsibilities will differ, depending on each project. However, the specific responsibilities should be listed in this section.

- Following the list of roles and responsibilities should be a matrix that displays the different types of tests, who is responsible for those tests, who is participating in those tests, and during what stage of the project those tests are put into action.

- The next section is the **Acceptance Testing Schedule** that lists each activity within the testing period, who is responsible and the due date

- The **fourth** chapter is the **Environment** section which will describe the testing site, who will be establishing the location, and any technical resources that are needed.

- The next section will list the **Resources** including personnel, locations, financial resources, tools, and any other resources that will be necessary to complete the testing process.

- The **fifth** chapter opens with the **Reporting** section, which identifies what kind of reports and/or records will be derived out of the testing process.

- Following the reporting section is the **Test Case Report,** which identifies how test reports will be collected and contains a list of any information that will be required for a test case.

- The **sixth** chapter contains information about **Testing Prerequisites.** It should include any events that must take place before acceptance testing occurs. This chapter will also include information about quality assurance, developing test cases, and how the test case data will be collected and presented.

- The **seventh** chapter is the **Testing Procedures** section. Most importantly, this chapter will contain the testing schedule, list the test results with their review, and will describe briefly any corrective action the team must take to improve the product. Following this, the team either accepts and releases the final output, or it halts the testing procedure to pursue a different testing approach.

The Communications Plan

The plan for acceptance testing is followed by the **communications plan**. The purpose of the communications plan is to help the project manager relay important information to important parties, such as shareholders, at important times.

A proper communications plan will convey the following information:

- What kind of information will be communicated and how?

- When will the information be communicated?

- Who will be communicating the information?

- What are the shareholders' responsibilities in communicating?

- What kind of resource allocation is available to put toward communications?

- Who will authorize and/or communicate sensitive information?

- Who will be managing any changes in the communications plan?

- Are there any restrictions to communication?

- How will issues and/or conflicts within the communications process be resolved?

Who's Your Audience?

One of the first steps in communication planning is to determine the project's **audience**. The audience usually consists of various groups of people you will be communicating with. The information you communicate and the way you communicate it depends on who you message is directed toward. The audience for a project in a large organization can be huge. It may include upper management, middle management, shareholders and even board members. The audience may change, depending on which specific part of the project is the issue. For example, part of the audience for acceptance testing can be the actual testers. You may be communicating with multiple audiences within each project, requiring several different messages, each containing a different level of information. For example, the technical audience will expect to receive a much different type of information from the audience involved in purchasing.

To clarify matters, you or your team will also identify the specific **information requirements** for each individual audience. For example, while the technical audience may not need to know the cost of certain resources, the purchasing audience will; however, it does not need design and development details.

Next, the team must determine *how* the information will be relayed. Project information is generally communicated through some form of **media.** Different audience members will prefer use of different forms of communication. In addition to basic contact information and the type of information you will need to pass on, you will need to record preferred forms of communication and specific contact identifiers (e.g., email address).

There are numerous media channels that can be used to communicate information. The most commonly used are email, newsletters, videos, presentations, meetings, webinars, and training sessions. The type of media the team will use to relay information may differ at times; some channels are not the best fit for certain situation. For example, email may be a great means to communicate project milestones, but it is not an effective way to communicate training information. A video may not be the most efficient way to communicate milestones and updates, but it works fine for training.

All of this information should be included in the communications plan, starting from the planning stage of the project. Although the information may not be fully developed at that point, it serves as a starting point; communications levels and contact information can be added to the plan as the information is received.

The communications plan should include a schedule of events. The team will have developed this during the communications planning process, with tasks assigned to each team member. The tasks and roles may change throughout the duration of the project but they should be laid out during this planning stage.

The Procurement Plan

The communications plan is followed by the final step in the planning process, which is the **procurement plan.** The objective of a procurement plan is to develop a process for fulfilling the project's need for resources in an efficient manner and at the most efficient costs. A procurement plan enables the purchasing process to be transparent and smooth as opposed to poorly planned and barely scraped together.

While the procurement plan is created during the planning stage, it will be revisited throughout the duration of the project. This plan is highly flexible; any adjustments that result in potential savings for the organization are welcomed. Procurement planning promotes transparency, building trust with outside parties and securing contracts quickly, minimizing costly delays, making it easier to attract the best suppliers and build stronger relationships with them.

There are two types of procurement plans: **consolidated procurement plans** and **individual procurement planning**. Consolidated procurement plans are usually created for the entire organization at a regional or divisional level and are often published for the benefit of multiple projects. Individual procurement planning consists of a procurement manager developing a plan for a single project. Individual plans usually focus on major expenditures that may be harder to secure than others.

Although the procurement process may not necessarily occur in this order, the first step is usually to define the procurement goals. The goals will serve as a framework to develop everything else in the process. The next step is to gather information, which consists of defining the procurement requirements and analyzing the supply market. Once that is completed, the team can then begin to develop the procurement plan itself.

The procurement plan generally includes:

- Procurement goals.

- Performance indicators.

- How the procurement activities mesh with the procurement strategy.

- Who is responsible for which activities.

- A procurement schedule with milestones.

- Any administrative requirements.

Chapter 3: Defining Project Success

One can define a successful project as one that meets or exceeds its requirements, is kept on track, is completed on time, and meets or exceeds its customers' expectations. A failed project is defined as anything that falls outside the realm of the definition of a successful project.

As you have learned by now and will continue to discover, there are multiple factors that contribute to a project's success. The last thing any project manager wants to do is lead a project into disaster or to mess up the budget, schedule, or any other important factor that can leave the project in ruins! However, there are a few important strategies that a great project manager can focus on to increase the chances of having a successful project run.

Goals

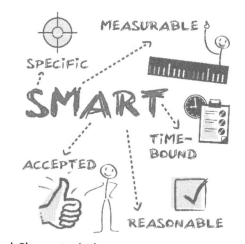

Goal Characteristics

It is important to establish clear goals for the project and to communicate them clearly with the team, shareholders, sponsors, and customers. Anyone who attempts any major feat without clear goals is only asking for trouble to follow difficulty. This becomes even more essential when your project turns out to be large and complex.

Goal setting breaks down large projects into smaller, more attainable pieces, so that the work can be ordered in the proper sequence. It allows you to take note of project steps that can be re-used and not re-created from scratch. Finally, the goal-setting process helps to reveal how the work can best be divided up to ensure that everything comes together successfully in the end.

The most important thing to remember about goals is that they must be clear, straightforward, to the point, and achievable, especially when you are laying down goals for a team effort. Everybody must be on the same page and have the same understanding of the expected results in order for goal setting to have an impact.

Plans

Planning is an essential prerequisite to the successful execution of project goals and their end objective. As we have already discussed, planning is a vital step in project management; it is probably as essential to the project as the work itself. Without the planning phase, a project lacks direction, clarity, focus, and the essential "how-tos" that allow a multi-disciplined team of individuals to coordinate their efforts toward a common end. If a project manager skips the planning stage, a project will more than likely fail. At the very least, its quality will suffer.

Quality

To know how to define a project's successful completion, it's important to define clearly, down to the finest detail, what the quality of the final output should look like. The planning process helps to clarify the level of precision required in the end product. While the details may be vague at the beginning of planning, as the project's expectations become more clearly defined, its quality requirements will become clearer. The higher the quality of the final result, the more finely the quality can be measured.

The earlier you define the specifics of product expectations, the easier it becomes to build concrete policies and procedures to achieve and measure that result. Quality objectives aren't limited to the end product itself. They will be established for each stage of the project completion, including each intermediate step along the way.

Realism

The planning and execution of a project requires everyone to have feet firmly planted on terra firma. At some point, all the schedules, budgets, resource requirement, strategies, and contingency planning become implemented in real life and reality sets in, big-time. Inevitably, there will be moments when reality does not mesh with any of your carefully crafted schedules, budgets, etc. This is where project management and clearly defined team roles and relationships can save the day.

A project manager who has a realistic mindset looks ahead to see contingencies coming and can engage the team in finding solutions, often before the contingency has a chance to unfold. Even when unexpected contingencies occur, the structure provided by the planning process will have laid a solid foundation to allow both project manager and team to find a way through the challenge, often without jeopardizing the forward momentum of the project.

Anticipating Change

A project is one massive process of challenging the status quo. After all, by creating an end project, the project itself is a singular instigator of change. Anticipating change can help keep a project grounded when the status quo is shaken up. Do you remember how important change management is in preventing scope creep? A project team that anticipates and adjusts smoothly to change is more likely to have a successful run than one that balks at any modifications.

Proactivity

Project managers who proactively address issues as they arise – if not before –are more likely to achieve success than those who procrastinate or ignore issues until the last minute. Taking immediate action on issues can save precious time and keep the project moving forward at a steady pace.

I've discovered that this applies to my personal life as well. Whenever an issue arises in my life, I take action as soon as I can to address it. That way, I don't find myself wasting time distractedly worrying about it when I could be turning my energies toward something more productive

Shareholder Communication

Project managers who effectively communicate with all the project stakeholders are much more likely to experience customer satisfaction in the end than those who provide only sporadic and partial status updates. Just think how you would feel if you're waiting on someone to finish a project you expect to change your life dramatically. The greater you think will be its impact on your life, the more interested you will be in its development, especially if you're paying for the project. The more your life will be affected, the more you will want a voice in the process.

Granted, different stakeholders have different interests. End users will be more interested in how the functionality is shaping up. Corporate sponsors will be primarily tuned into the financials, how the project will improve the bottom line and how much the project is costing them. Contributing vendors will require clear communication regarding what they are expected to provide and will want feedback regarding the quality of their contributions. They'll also expect payment eventually, so keeping them apprised of how things are progressing will offer a form of reassurance that, yes, they will be paid, sometime in the foreseeable future.

Team Size

Successful project managers know how to develop a perfectly-sized team. Their team must fit the project, in size as well as in skills. As the project takes shape, the roles needed for the task will become more clearly defined. As necessary, you will go looking for team members to fill those functional needs, whether within the organization or by hiring externally.

When the above aspects come into play, you'll have your hands full, if you are the project manager! While you are busy overseeing your project, here are some things to steer clear of:

Avoid Micromanaging.

Project managers who micromanage their teams are less likely to see success than those who allow their team members space to work independently. While it is important to communicate with team members and keep your finger on the pulse of the team, it is equally important to give the members room to do their jobs.

Don't Rely on Emails.

While email is an acceptable way to communicate formally with team members, shareholders, sponsors, and customers, it is important to remember that other modes of communication have their purposes, too. Email can be fine for sending out brief updates. However, face-to-face meetings and phone calls can be effective and efficient when passing on bulkier and more complicated information.

Email is not the place for offering constructive criticism; that should always be done face to face. A group forum would be much more effective when you need to work out key project strategies. If it's important to be certain that your team members have heard and understood complex information, you may send them a document via email ahead of time, but a follow-up group meeting is the most efficient and effective way to answer questions and address concerns. Messaging, on the other hand is usually a faster way to send a simple question and get back a swift response.

Don't Treat Your Team Like Robots

One mistake project managers sometimes make is to forget that their team is made up of human beings, replete with emotions, thoughts, feelings, and the occasional mistake. Project managers who act as if their team members are super-human, or non-human, are just asking for project failure. Great project managers know that valuing their team players and honoring their contributions is the key to success.

Don't Lose Sight of Priorities

Another mistake project managers sometimes make is to set urgent tasks above important tasks. It's important to recognize the difference between the two. Careful planning, clear scope definition, and appropriate task scheduling can help to balance these priorities.

Don't Forget to Ask for Feedback.

Although it may seem more commonplace for project managers to give feedback to their team members, don't forget that it is equally important to receive feedback from your team as well. Without feedback and constructive criticism, it is impossible for a project manager to grow in skill and develop as a well-rounded human. If you don't listen to your team, you also erect a barrier wall that will ultimately prevent you from working effectively with your team. The job may get done, but the process will be draining instead of rewarding for those who work on it.

Don't Avoid Planning.

Although it may be tempting to breeze through the planning stage without giving it much thought, this is a sure recipe for project catastrophe. It is important to take the time to complete the adequate research, reach out to experts for their insights, and listen carefully to the wisdom of those who instigated the project in the first place. In a multitude of expert counselors lie the seeds of your project's success.

Avoid Rigidity

While having a plan is extremely important, it is also important to be flexible. This is the only way to weather the storms of unexpected change. Those unexpected contingencies demand flexibility if your project is to survive. They can wreak havoc on schedules and budgets. A great project manager will remain open to ideas for improvement and embrace any opportunity to recover lost time and dollars.

Now that you know what *not* to do, let's turn our attention to the qualities and skills a project manager *must* have in order to succeed on the job.

Chapter 4: The Qualities of a Great Project Manager

All projects, large or small, require the guidance of a project manager. This person does not usually participate directly in the work of the project. Instead, the project manager oversees the project as a whole, helping it stay on track toward its objectives, heading off potential problems, minimizing overhead, and staying within budget.

Some of the responsibilities of a project manager are to:

- Recruit and develop a diverse and efficient team.

- Assign tasks to each team member and oversee their progress.

- Identify efficient, easy to understand and realistic project objectives, then communicate them to the team.

- Explain the importance of the project.

- Oversee any procurement of staff, materials, technology, or anything else required for the completion of a successful project.

- Set the standards for the project's output.

- Manage the limitations of the project's scope, quality, and schedule.

- Promote a healthy team environment.

- Estimate the resources that are needed and schedule their provision.

- Perform risk assessments and monitor project changes.

- Manage shareholder expectations.

- Ultimately, close the project.

Project managers are the first person anyone will turn to in the event of a constraint, a project roadblock, or any other issue outside of the individual's authority to resolve.

Many project managers have special educational backgrounds and certifications that make them more effective in their work and, frankly, make them more appealing to possible employers. Some of these certifications include the Project Management Professional (PMP), the Certified Associate in Project Management (CAPM), the Program Management Professional (PgMP) and the Scheduling Professional (PMI-SP). Most of these certifications are offered by the Project Management Institute in the United States. There are also multiple organizations throughout the world that offer comparable certifications.

Characteristics Of A Project Manager

The above list of responsibilities only implies indirectly what it takes to be a project manager. A seasoned project manager has internal qualities that equip him or her to respond appropriately in any circumstance, for the well-being of the team and the advancement of the project.

A Great Project Manager Has a Vision.

A great project manager always has a specific vision of where he or she wants to go and at the same time has the ability to communicate that vision to the team. Having a vision means that you're open to change and you're willing to go where you've never gone before. Project managers with a vision are able to inspire their team members to act out their vital role within the team. An effective project manager with a powerful vision is "contagious", spreading inspiration and motivation to the rest of the team. He or she often motivates team members to create their own visions and work on turning those visions into reality.

A Great Project Manager is Selective with Data.

A great project manager must be able to skim quickly through data, knowing what to look for, what to ignore and what might require a response. Most projects yield tons of data, not all of which is important to the immediate needs of the project. A project manager who knows what to look for in the sea of data is able to detect potential problems there as well as identifying successes.

A Great Project Manager is a Skilled Communicator.

A great project manager is able to communicate clearly important information about goals, expectations, responsibilities and constructive feedback, to the team members. This person is also responsible for communicating with project sponsors about the progress of the project. It calls for tact, diplomacy, persuasion, a sense of timing, and negotiating skills to navigate the project toward success. According to the Project Management Institute, an ideal project manager should spend almost 100% of the time communicating with others, whether with team members, vendors, sponsors, or the ultimate end-users.

A Great Project Manager Listens and Asks the Right Questions.

As a skilled communicator, a great project manager must be able to ask the right questions when it comes to communicating with shareholders. Listening skills are equally valuable. Each person you communicate with has his or her own needs, interests, and fears; with a careful ear, you will be able to tailor your communications to speak directly to those concerns.

A Great Project Manager Practices Integrity.

A great project manager always practices honesty and good faith. Since he or she is essentially the leader of the group, the manager must set an example for the team. As the representative to those on the outside of the project, it is all the more important to be transparently honest. The project manager must be ethical and loyal and should always follow through on promises. A project manager who practices integrity ultimately earns the additional title of "trustworthy."

A Great Project Manager is Organized.

A great project manager must have impeccable organization skills. The best time to begin organizing your life around a project is at the very start, when you have the most available free time. It's generally a bad idea to wait until the middle of a project to start thinking about personal organization. In the throes of project execution, the schedule is often hectic and unpredictable, so the earlier you can set your personal procedures in place, the better.

A Great Project Manager Is Passionate.

A great project manager must remain passionate and excited about achieving a successful output. You must have a top-notch attitude and should never give up hope for a successful finish. Passionate project managers always focus on achieving their goals and they know how to sustain a positive attitude even in the event of unexpected challenges. The project manager's passion is infectious; it will usually spread to the rest of the team.

A Great Project Manager is a Motivator.

A great project manager must be skilled at motivating others. When it comes to figuring out how to motivate a team, there is no right answer. It usually flows from your personality. You tailor your motivation to speak to the personalities of your team members. If you can learn how to do this early on, you increase the chances of seeing great results and experiencing a smooth project run.

A Great Project Manager Is Empathetic.

A great project manager must know how to show empathy and compassion. It's easy, in the heat of battle, to forget that other people have lives outside of work, that they are not robots who never need a break. When you keep in mind the energy level and the stressors on the team, your awareness creates an opportunity to strengthen relationships as you act to provide space for these human needs.

A Great Project Manager Anticipates the Future.

While project managers are not psychic, a great project manager must be able to logically think ahead to anticipate what will happen down the road. If a project manager can detect early signs of an unforeseen contingency on the horizon and find a way to handle it early on, disaster can be averted and the project can continue to move forward. This calls for the opposite of procrastination. Instead of running away from trouble, the project manager must run directly toward it.

A Great Project Manager is Competent.

A great project manager must be competent. This does not mean that you must have all the skills called for by the project, but you must be able to lead competently a team that possesses those skills. You must be able to listen to the wisdom of your team and be willing to adjust the project accordingly. Your team members were chosen for their subject-matter expertise so don't hesitate to rely on it. Your job as project manager is to utilize your project management abilities to make the most of your team's various skills.

A Great Project Manager is Analytical.

A great project manager must be reasonably analytical, but not too much so. Some managers spend too much time analyzing, leading to delays in the project due to indecision. A great project manager must know how much time to spend on analysis, what needs to be analyzed in the first place, and what doesn't need your scrutiny because it will work itself out in the process.

A Great Project Manager Knows How To Delegate.

A great project manager knows the team members well enough to delegate tasks efficiently, based on individual technical skills and personal abilities. Delegation also reveals trust in the team members. As you appropriately delegate key tasks to your team, their trust in you – and in their teammates' abilities – will increase.

A Great Project Manager Is A Master Negotiator.

A great project manager must also be a great negotiator. This skill 7set is important for occasions where there might be a disagreement between two or more team members. The project manager is responsible for resolving disagreements as agreeably as possible. You also want to anticipate possible objections and handle them behind the scenes if possible, to avoid negatively affecting the team's synergy.

A Great Project Manager Maintains Composure.

A great project manager must be able to maintain emotional composure in the event of any difficulty. Many projects come with a high amount of pressure; if something goes wrong, it's easy for the project manager to feel overwhelmed. However, it is important to remain calm and confident, for the sake of your team and the many stakeholders that are constantly watching.

Great project managers are able to look at problems as challenges rather than the end of the world. They view trouble as an opportunity to do what they're there for – facilitating workable solutions and minimizing any impact on the project, its physical resources, and the project team.

A Great Project Manager is a Planner.

A great project manager always has a plan. Part of the planning process is used to prioritize the most important tasks of the project. Planning is important because it reduces your chances of running into unexpected obstacles. The project manager is the best person to oversee the prioritization of tasks because he or she should know exactly what the project requires for a successful conclusion.

A Great Project Manager is a Team Builder.

A great project manager must be able to build a solid team. Teams usually start out as a bunch of people who don't know each other. By the end of the project, however, they will have become a highly effective working group. The project manager must be able to help these people mesh together as a functioning team and lead them toward a common goal.

Managing the Team Lifecycle

There are five stages of development during the life of any team. Entering a stage marks progress in a team's ability to work together. Each new stage also presents fresh challenges for the project manager, as each stage requires the team members to deal with a fresh set of challenges. During each stage, it is up to the leader to take action to facilitate the team individuals' successful navigation of these challenges.

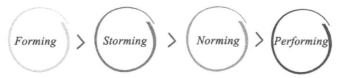

The Team Life Cycle

Here is how a project manager serves the team through each stage of the team's life:

- The **forming** stage begins when team members come together for the first time. They may know each other from previous interactions, or this may be the first time they ever set eyes on each other. If they are strangers, the advantage is that they don't have any negative baggage to lug into the relationship. Of course, the disadvantage is, they don't have any past *positive* memories of working together effectively.

Different personalities respond to meeting new people differently. Some people love it; others hate it; few people are unaffected by the change. Even if part of the team has worked together before, the team itself is new, the project is new, and therefore, the team dynamics are going to be new. Consequently, it is the responsibility of the team leader to set the emotional tone of the team, to establish basic guidelines for working together, and to affirm the value each team member to the rest of the team.

At this point, as project manager, you are the "glue" that holds the team together; you are one thing they all have in common. Even if the personalities are vastly different, the project itself can serve as their common ground. It's your job to help them see eye to eye on their common purpose. It might be necessary at the beginning to defend the project to the team; you may be called to win everybody over to the value of the project. Ultimately, you need not just their agreement in writing, but their personal commitment to work as part of this team to accomplish the stated objective.

- The **storming** stage occurs as the team transitions from random individuals into a functioning team. The work begins and personalities inevitably clash. As the leader of the pack, it is your responsibility to serve as the mediator when the parties can't come to an agreement. You can often see trouble on the horizon and take initiative to head it off before a storm can arise to threaten progress.

  During this stage, productivity may well suffer, but the storming must take place if you want a strong, resilient team. You will want to consistently affirm the value of each team member during this period. You will probably spend time calming anxieties, reducing fears, and listening to frustrations. This is the stage where the team members learn what each other is made of and work out the most effective ways to work together. Feel free to provide gentle guidance, periodically. Definitely step in to avert total meltdown, but for the most part, let the team storm around you, even *with* you as necessary, until they have come to a useful working arrangement.

- You will know that your team has reached the **norming** stage when it begins to get along and production picks up again. As a leader, you will probably not have to do much during this stage except work alongside your team, provide minor course corrections, and keep up with the paperwork and communications.

- The norming stage transitions into the **performing** stage as your team begins to seriously make progress. Your team will be working synergistically with each other and they will usually work their own way through any problems or issues that arise.

As a project leader, you must strategically delegate tasks during the performing stage. You can also offer feedback to team members to affirm their work and help them work even more effectively. You'll spend key time interacting with team members during this stage, celebrating their successes with them and keeping an eye out for ways to facilitate the work.

By the time you reach this stage, you should be familiar with how your team works and thinks. When you get inside of your team's "head," it can really help you with finding out what motivates them and what doesn't. You can tailor your rewards to match what blesses them the most.

- Once the objective is reached and all the work is completed, your team will shift into the unofficial but nevertheless very real **disbanding** stage. You can facilitate the progress through this phase by marking project completion with a special celebration. Give the whole team an opportunity to relax and have fun together, celebrate their accomplishments, express gratitude for all the good times, and to show appreciation for the friendships that have developed during this project.

    Team members are dealing emotionally and mentally with the ending of an era. You can help by giving them what time and space you can to process the impending change, before you return them to their former lives.

A Great Project Manager is Adaptable.

A great project manager must easily adapt to all situations. If you're unwilling to embrace change, you limit your potential to lead the project and all its people toward a successful project ending.

If change terrifies you, this will probably be the first character trait you need to work on. Each time you choose to embrace change and walk forward, head up into it, you practice the adaptability that is so essential whenever you find yourself in a new situation.

A Great Project Manager is a Problem Solver.

A great project manager must be a skilled problem solver. This requires the ability to solve any type of problem alone, or with the help of the team. There must be enough trust between the project manager and the team for the manager to solve problems directly, but it is important to involve the rest of the team when possible.

A Great Project Manager is Self-Motivated.

In addition to being able to motivate others, the project manager must possess a generous portion of self-motivation. If you're having trouble finding reasons to motivate yourself to lead your team, one thing you can do is ask yourself why you decided to become a project manager. Asking yourself "why" will usually generate answers that are very meaningful to you. Meaningful answers often lead to reasons for self-motivation. For example, you may have become a project manager to provide for your family. So when you meet with your team and then come across a roadblock and you feel like giving up, you can remind yourself that you're doing it for your family and then you will probably feel less likely to want to quit.

A Great Project Manager is Confident.

A great project manager consistently displays confidence. As a project manager you are also a leader and if your team sees that you aren't confident then a lack of confidence is likely to spread to your team as well. Although we all strive to have happy and positive days, the reality is that everyone runs into bad days here and there. When that happens to you, don't let it affect your confidence and thus your ability to do your job. Being confident can positively impact your team and it will most likely make your team look forward to working together. Even if you do find it difficult to remain confident in times of trouble, act like you're a super hero and assume that you will succeed regardless. Have you ever heard the term "fake it until you make it?" Some of the most successful leaders have acted fearless in times of peril and succeeded!

A Great Project Manager Has a Great Attitude.

A great project manager is positive at all times. Staying positive includes everything from not letting challenges discourage you to encouraging your teammates to actively looking for things to praise. When your employees come to you with a problem, whether work-related or personal, feed their hope first, and then facilitate their thinking as they work things through to reach a workable solution.

A Great Project Manager is Solution-Driven.

A great project manager is always ready to find a new solution. The worst mistake you could make is to assume that you will never run into a roadblock in your work. Even if you are the most driven project manager you will eventually run into a couple of snags throughout your career. A solution-driven project manager always looks at roadblocks and obstacles as a learning experience and a challenge to improve his or her skills. Never give up until you find a solution! Successful leaders start from a standpoint of hope, confident that there is a way out. They view it as their job to find that way and pursue it.

A Great Project Manager Is Self-leading

A great project manager doesn't rely on the hundreds of books, courses, and seminars to teach leadership style, although those have their place. He or she relies on self-leadership to inspire his or her followers to follow suit. To be a self-leader you must first establish a sense of identity. For example, you have to develop your strengths and work on improving your weaknesses before you can begin leading a team.

A Great Project Manager is Consistent.

A great project manager responds consistently to people and circumstances. Consistency is an outgrowth of being confident, organized, and committed to leading an operation. It inspires others to trust you and encourages their faith in your general fairness. For example, if you trained your team on the quality level required to complete one part of a project, they will only be motivated to reach that level themselves if you sustain a high level of quality in *your* work. Your work ethic and consistent quality performance both model and establish the work environment for the entire team.

A Great Project Manager Speaks Professionally.

A great project manager is articulate and professional when discussing the project. You speak respectfully of and to others. When your speech is logical and grammatically correct, it lends weight to your words. People take you seriously and respect your authority in the role of project manager when you convey your respect for the position.

You'll want to speak slowly enough for people to understand you; also, limit your technical terminology to conversations with people who understand those terms. Pay careful attention to your audience and choose your words to speak directly to their interests and concerns.

A Great Project Manager Has Great Writing Skills.

In addition to verbal communication skills, a great project manager must also be a good writer. As you have discovered, there are many aspects of project management that require excellent writing skills. In the professional world, you must know how to properly write emails, memos and other important documents that will serve as communication bridges between you, your team, the stakeholders and anyone else involved in the project.

If you struggle with spelling or grammar, chances are somebody on your team will excel in this arena; there is no reason you can't ask a trusted person to proofread your communiqués before you send them out. You want to present yourself professionally in this respect as well, so don't rely on computer-based word checking; when in doubt ask an expert.

A Great Project Manager is Skilled with Technology.

A great project manager is always up to date on the latest technology in the field. Technology can help you advance your project and improve your management skills. When used correctly, technology is a great way to help efficiently lead a project.

A Great Project Manager Can Train Others.

A great project manager needs some training experience. When you train others you are modeling how the team members can equip each other in valued skills. The more diverse your team's skills, the better your team will be equipped to help each other out as needed to move the project forward. Training your team members on new skills can not only make them feel great but it can also make your project run more efficiently and strengthen the relationships within your group. When you're a great trainer, those you have trained often always have great things to say about you and it is likely that you will develop a strong reputation as a successful leader.

A Great Project Manager Knows How to Build Rapport.

A great project manager must be skilled at building rapport with others. By finding common ground with others that you've never met before, you can easily find ways to "hit it off" with each other. Imitating body language such as making eye contact or matching your partner's body language is a good way to build rapport and thus gain trust. You can also ask questions such as, "Oh you like gardening? Me too!" to find common ground. When you find common ground with another person it makes it so much easier to genuinely connect with each other. Using these techniques can help strengthen the bonds between you and your teammates and amongst your teammates to increase trust and synergy.

A Great Project Manager Practices Time Management.

A mature project manager has impeccable time management skills. Not practicing time management can have a negative impact on productivity. When you practice excellent time management skills you will find that you have more time to complete more tasks. When you put great time management skills into practice, your team will too. Time management is so important to the field of project management that I've devoted the entire next chapter to giving you strategies that will boost your proficiency in this area

A Great Project Manager Knows The Team Inside Out.

One of the responsibilities of the team manager is to delegate tasks, but you can only delegate tasks effectively, if you know the capabilities of your team. As you get to know your team you will become increasingly aware of which members have what abilities and interests, and you will grow increasingly effective at assigning people the work they can shine at and enjoy. Productivity soars as people are able to thrive and do well.

A Great Project Manager Is Available.

A great project manager is available to the team at all times. As a leader, you know that time is an important but limited resource. An important part of your job is to give your team members the time they need with you. To be a successful project facilitator, your team needs to know that they will receive your full attention when they approach you, even if they just need reassurance that they are doing okay.

A Great Project Manager Genuinely Cares for the Team.

Genuinely caring for your team members can help you become a great project manager. Some leaders focus on their own business, forgetting that it's the people who work for them who cause it to thrive. Caring for your team members can increase the overall level of team morale. If your team members believe that you genuinely care for them, they will be much more likely to respond willingly to extra requests.

A Great Project Manager Has Fun.

Last but not least, don't forget to have fun! Nothing is worse than working a job that makes you miserable. If you show that you are having fun, your team will feel able to have fun as well. There is such thing as being able to have fun while still being professional and getting things done. Play is an important aspect of supporting team morale and creating an inviting workplace, all key responsibilities of your job. If you can bring a light heart to work, it'll infect those you work with and around.

Chapter 5: Time Management Strategies

Time management is one of the most essential skills for running a successful project. The practice of time management is key to reaching your goals and completing milestones on time. These, in turn, are what keep the project on track and on schedule. Time management includes communicating efficiently with shareholders. Because time is money, especially when it comes to project execution, your skills as a time manager can make – or break – your career.

Goals, milestones and other deadlines are developed during the planning process with the idea that the project manager and team will use time management tactics to complete them on time. Throughout the project, the project manager monitors all events to ensure that they are progressing within the projected time parameters. If they stray outside those guidelines, it's the work of the project manager to find a work-around to prevent the entire project from falling behind schedule.

The best way to develop a time management plan for your project is to model it off past successful projects. The team will look for specific objectives in the project charter and break down the process of reaching them into manageable tasks that can be prioritized and assigned a due date. It's also helpful to try and allocate some extra time for each task in the event of contingencies. There is no one formula for assigning time limits; they are usually worked out by the team, depending on the individual project. The only date that's decided on outside of the team is the final deadline, which involves the opinion of the shareholders. Once each task has been broken down, prioritized, and assigned a due date, each team member is allocated specific tasks to complete.

The project manager is responsible for the time management of actual events as well as documenting the time allocation process. As noted in the planning process, the project manager is also responsible for estimating the types and amounts of resources necessary to create a schedule of events.

According to the Project Management Institute, here are the main tools needed to execute time management:

Schedule Network Analysis

A schedule network analysis is the formal term for creating the project's schedule. A project schedule will contain a **schedule network diagram**, a visual representation of each task, showing where various tasks are interconnected. This is the same network diagram we talked about when we were discussing the planning stage, back in Chapter 2. In this case it is used for the purpose of scheduling resources.

One of the most important aspects of schedule network analysis is the opportunity to identify **project slack**. This consists of pinpointing the earliest and latest dates a task can without compromising the project.

There are multiple ways to look at network analysis:

- The **Critical Path Method (CPM)** uses a schedule network diagram to find the project's critical path or shortest possible time to completion. This identifies the shortest elapsed time in which your project can be finished. With this method, the late completion of a task that lies along the critical path will cause a delay in project completion, since there is no lag time allowed between tasks.

- The **Critical Chain Method** focuses on the resources available at any given time along the project path. Not only do you need to know when tasks can be started, you also want to know if you have the manpower and equipment necessary to take on the task in the allotted amount of time.

- The **What-If Scenario Analysis (WISA)** allows the project manager to experiment with tweaking variables to see how it would affect things like cost and project completion date.

- The **Resource Leveling Method** tries to balance out the way you use resources for a project, in an attempt to minimize overhead costs.

Schedule Compression

Schedule compression is a technique that project managers can use in the event that a project schedule is overwhelmed with tasks or if the project needs to be adjusted to a faster pace. In other words, a schedule compression is an attempt to make the project shorter without making any changes to the scope. Usually it is used to meet a deadline or to catch up from missing a previous deadline. There are two very important sub-techniques in schedule compression:

- **Fast Tracking** involves re-prioritizing tasks so that some of them can be worked in parallel, instead of sequentially. The purpose is to gain time. Sometimes a task can be broken down and parts of it completed simultaneously. Some portions can be started before others are completed. Depending on the nature of the project, fast tracking can be accomplished without generating extra cost, but extra care must be taken to ensure that nothing gets missed in the process of breaking up the tasks.

- **Crashing** – If fast tracking hasn't gained enough time, crashing may help speed the process. It involves pressing into service extra resources that weren't included in the original budget, trading off money and manpower for time. The theory is that more resources will make for a faster project (e.g., the more people who work on a task, the faster it will be completed). This can work, but if the expertise of the individuals pressed into service varies, the gains may be spotty.

Schedule Controls

A schedule control is the process of continuously monitoring the progress of the work, constantly comparing the current state to the planned schedule. It involves frequently evaluating whether anything is causing the schedule to run ahead or behind and tweaking things to keep things progressing as smoothly as possible.

There are four steps to schedule control:

- **Analysis** – The project manager begins by analyzing the actual timeframes of each task, comparing the actual progress against the scheduled progress. The purpose is to identify schedule overruns as they occur, or even earlier if possible.

- **Correction** – The project manager chooses corrective strategies and sets in motion their implementation. These corrections could range from a minor tweak or brief reassignment of tasks, to a total revamping of the schedule, a **revision**.

- **Revision** – If minor resource reallocation doesn't solve the problem, the project manager revamps the schedule, using fast tracking or crashing as warranted. The objective is to fit the remaining tasks back within the project timeframe.

- **Re-Evaluation** – Finally, the project manager reviews the modified schedule to ensure that that it continues to meet efficiency and quality requirements despite the changes. If necessary, the correction, revision, and re-evaluation steps can be reiterated until a satisfactory schedule emerges.

Time Management Tools for Project Managers

While there are many great time management strategies for personal and business purposes, several strategies have been developed to answer specific needs within project management.

Activity Logs

Activity logs are just that; they are tools you can use to keep track of the work as it is performed, gaining a visual representation of how time resources are distributed across each task. Activity logs are meant for logging the progress of individuals. They are much more efficient than relying solely on your memory, which is already crammed full of important information and churning to solve problems.

Many project managers who use these tools for the first time are surprised at how much down time exists in a project. You can also use activity logs to identify which times of the day are the most productive and which team members seem to make greatest progress on which sort of tasks.

Once you've logged the team's activities for a couple of days, you can study them to look for areas to make improvements. Massive improvements can be realized immediately by eliminating or reducing the time spent on tasks not directly related to the success of the project.

Many successful teams and project managers use activity logs to schedule their most important tasks during the times when they perform at their best. Because work expands to fill the amount of time allotted to it, you can also use the log to compress the amount of time you spend on a task.

Precedence Diagrams

One of the best ways to determine precedence within a project is to use the precedence diagram method (PDM). The PDM is a scheduling tool that identifies the dependency of individual activities within a project.

There are numerous benefits to using a precedence diagram:

- The diagram can make it easier to communicate the flow of a project to the team and the shareholders.

- It can help point out missing activities in the sequence, or items that are out of sequence based on their dependencies.

- It highlights dependencies so that any potential project delays are significantly decreased.

- It highlights any activities that are critical to keeping the project on schedule; this can help project managers determine the critical path of the project.

- It can serve as the first step to creating a schedule.

Using a precedence diagram to identify the correct dependencies between project activities is important, because if it is not done correctly it can delay the project's completion. A precedence diagram enables project managers to see these dependencies.

There are four main types of dependencies between any two activities:

- **Finish to Start**: In this dependency relationship, the second activity cannot begin until the first activity is completely finished. This is the most common dependency type. In a perfect world, there would be enough time and resources to run a strictly sequential project using finish to start dependencies. However, the use of resources is often restricted; shortened project deadlines often make it necessary to double up on tasks wherever possible. The following dependency types allow some of the tasks to be telescoped down slightly.

- **Start to Start**: This dependency means that the first activity must start before the second activity can start. For

example, I must start writing down my questions before you can begin to respond to them (unless, of course, we're playing "Jeopardy").

- **Finish to Finish**: In this case, the first activity must finish before the second activity can finish. For example, you must finish writing a book before your editor can finish editing it. This implies that the editing work can be started while the writing is still in progress.

- **Start to Finish**: The second activity must start before the first activity can finish. This type of dependency is rarely used. An example of this relationship would be a data systems migration, where the second system must be up and running before the first system can be shut down.

Gantt Charts

Gantt Chart

A Gantt chart is a visual representation of how tasks are scheduled over time. A typical Gantt chart will look like a series of horizontal bars, showing scheduled start and end dates, arranged in the order of when they start. This is an ideal tool for small to medium-sized projects with multiple people working on them. They're easy to create using a spreadsheet, or you can use software designed to facilitate the process. You can quickly see places where the project is ahead or behind schedule by comparing the current status of the various activities with the visual bars on the Gantt chart.

As with anything, there are advantages and disadvantages to using Gantt charts. They make it easy to organize tasks by priority, start or end time, and responsibility. Their format is easy to read and understand. Gantt charts are great tools for breaking tasks down into specific time frames. However, they aren't as useful for large-scale projects, because they can't adequately represent the complexity of task relationships.

Action Checklists

Action checklists are a list of tasks that you need to complete to achieve a goal. You may have multiple checklists for a large goal that is broken down into smaller sub-goals. Creating an action checklist can enable you to think through each step of your goal most thoroughly.

To create an action plan, all you do is list each task in the order you need to complete it. Action checklists can assist you in keeping track of your goals and provide a means to record updated goals.

To-Do Lists

This may sound like a no-brainer, but project managers find to-do lists extremely helpful in managing their time and the time requirements of the whole project. One of the most important principles of time management is to know everything that needs to get done before you start doing it; to-do lists provide a visual aid to keep you aware of all those necessary tasks. To-do lists can help you remember the smallest of details and they can provide a realistic view of how much work you have ahead of you. The perspective it provides can reduce procrastination, help you prioritize your work, motivate you to press on to complete the list, and can help you set realistic time management goals. To-do lists are easily written down, but they can just as easily be stored on your phone, tablet, or computer for easy reference.

To make the most out of your to-do list, assign an estimated time limit to each task. This can make a huge difference in your time management. If you've never done before, your time estimates may be wildly unrealistic at first, but the more you practice this, the more accurate they will become.

Once you have set down time estimations for each task, add it up and then divide by the amount of time you have to complete them; this will help you schedule tasks in the most efficient manner possible. It's also important to prioritize each task on your to-do list to make sure that the most important tasks get done first. You'll want to leave some wiggle room in your work schedule to allow for unexpected difficulties and estimations that didn't allow enough time to complete the work.

To-do lists can be especially helpful in helping you see where you need to break a large task into smaller, more manageable sub-tasks. If you check off items as they are completed, it will provide instant positive feedback during the day, showing your progress and adding motivation to keep on pressing forward.

Time Management Strategies

Aside from specific project management tools and techniques for time management, project managers benefit from having good time management skills in general. Here are some excellent time management strategies you can practice to boost your time management skills.

Delegate Tasks

One thing that I have learned throughout life is that it is impossible for one person to do everything by him or herself. Not only is doing everything on your own nearly impossible, it brings down your productivity and just isn't efficient at all. The whole point of having a project management team is so that each team member can bring a certain skill or strength to the table so that when everyone works together, the project runs smoothly and can be very successful!

Don't Sit Still

Sitting still, at a desk for example, can put a damper on your time management skills. This is because non-movement drains your energy levels and when your energy levels are low, it is much harder to get things done in an efficient manner. Sitting is overall bad for our health in general, so if you can, come up with some ways to get your team moving around so that they're not sitting for hours on end. You might even agree to take breaks throughout the day between each task and encourage your team members to go for a walk outside, grab a quick healthy snack or to do a little bit of light stretching. Always wait to complete a task in full before taking a break. That way, when everyone comes back together, they can focus their minds on the next thing and easily concentrate.

Another idea you could try is to encourage fidgeting. If you have access to swivel chairs, you can swivel around while still keeping your eyes focused on your task at hand. Don't be afraid to stretch your legs, move your ankles around or strength upwards in your chair. You might also be open to idea of allowing your team to use fidget spinners, fidget cubes or any other device that is made to allow fidgeting. These items have become very popular over the last couple of months. I have a fidget spinner myself and I've found that it can really help me concentrate and it's not a distraction at all when used quietly.

Get Rid of Real Distractions

There are many distractions in our lives and they are mostly technological. For example, we are nearly surrounded by smart phones, tablets, computers, TVs and social media channels all day long, all of which are easily distracting. I don't know about you but when I open up Facebook, sometimes I get so absorbed into it that hours pass by before I know it! While most of this technology is really great and helpful, it's no lie that it can be very distracting, especially when we need to be focusing on something else. The best solution is to disconnect from all distractions while focusing on your project or any other task at hand.

Disconnecting is relatively easy. It can be as simple as turning off your phone, unplugging your TV, removing batteries from a device or uninstalling apps. Best of all, there's no need to worry about losing your information or data when you turn these things off, alieving yourself of all distractions completely.

One thing that many leaders are likely to be distracted by is checking email. Checking your email is as easy as ever because most mobile devices are now equipped with email apps that let you check your email at the touch of your fingers. While checking your email is important for staying in communication with people such as your team and stakeholders, I recommend limiting your email checking to three times per day. You could put aside a certain time to check your emails, such as during breaks. Another idea is to program your phone to receive pop-up notifications from your emailing app. This way you can take a quick glance at your phone to see whether an email is important or not by looking at the subject line.

Keep Your Concentration

Focusing on only one task at a time is critical for being productive. Finish each task fully before moving on to the next one. Going back and forth between tasks or experiencing multiple interruptions can cause you to forget important points of your task, thus causing you to have to spend more time on it. When you are interrupted from a task, there's only a 20% chance that you'll get to go back to it with ultimate concentration so always try to get each task done from beginning to end. If noise is a concern, a pair of earplugs or a set of noise-cancelling headphones can easily do the trick.

No!

This may be hard for some people but to be more productive it is important to say "no!" when you have too. Saying no to your boss, family or close friends can be very difficult but as long as you find the right way to say it, you will find that it's not too hard. A good way to say no to something without feeling bad is to explore alternative options. For example, if your family wants you to hang out with them but you've got a ton of work to get done you could agree on a better time to get together.

It is important to ensure that you take care of your personal needs first; otherwise you will really find yourself drained of energy and unable to fulfil any kind of request. For example, don't allow a request to trump taking a nap or taking the time to eat something.

Set Attainable Goals

Goal-setting is a great strategy for maximizing your productivity. Not only is goal-setting important for breaking down your largest tasks and working piece-by-piece to success, it can also increase your motivation. Every time you achieve a piece of your goal you can view it as a small success that will eventually bring you to ultimate success. As you continue to set and achieve goals, your mind will automatically begin anticipating success rather than failure.

Goal-setting is really easy! However, achieving your goals is a little tougher due to daily distractions and the temptation of procrastination. However, there are some tips you can follow to make it easier.

- Review what you've accomplished at the end of each day. This way you can see what you've already achieved and what you have left. Use time at the end of the day to plan out how you will continue to work toward achieving your goals the next day.

- Simply reviewing your goals once per day can help you concentrate on achievement.

- If you're a procrastinator, identify the root cause of your distractions. Of course, we all have "off" days and may find that some days we just may not have what it takes to put 100% focus toward reaching our goals. When this happens, just pick one or two simple things you can do toward your overall goal. By doing this, you're still working toward achievement but not overwhelming yourself at the same time.

- Avoid making excuses, as they will get you nowhere but in a circle.

- Work through your fears and don't let them stand in the way of allowing you to achieve your goals! Remember that nobody makes any huge accomplishments overnight – you will need to give yourself time to learn how to overcome your fears. However, avoid using your fears as your motivation. It's actually very unproductive and can potentially hold you back from success. Instead of focusing on your fears, focus on all the good things that will follow doing a good job.

- If your goal involves something that it new to you, allow yourself to make mistakes. Again, mistakes can only help you improve as long as you don't allow them to bring your confidence and attitude down. When you do start to get the hang of something new, don't forget to reward yourself!

- Find an accountability partner. When you want to achieve something, tell somebody who you can trust to hold you accountable. When you tell someone you're going to do something, you're more likely to actually do it because you know that somebody is holding you accountable for your actions. It can also help boost your focus and motivation.

- Don't forget to give yourself credit for all of your hard work. A good way to do this is to give yourself a reward when you accomplish mini-achievements. A reward gives you something to look forward to and can motivate you to work faster and harder. For example, if you've turned off all of your electronics during your focus period, your reward might be to turn them back on. You could also give yourself much bigger rewards for achieving huge successes, such as planning a cruise.

Chapter 6: Finishing Well

The final stage of the project management process is closure, which indicates the completion of the project and the achievement of the final objective. At this point, you will have delivered, or will be ready to deliver, the output you promised to the shareholders; you will have met all your goals.

Closing out a project means that you have met all of the acceptance standards and that the shareholders are happy with the results. It involves handing over the final result, whether a physical product or a service, to those who have sponsored the project.

There's an art to closing down a project. You don't just pack away all the information and documents, never to be seen again. You certainly don't want to go diving into a new project without getting proper closure on the current one.

Project closure entails some important steps. Like almost every other aspect of the project, it's possible to run into obstacles in the process. You'll want to be prepared to face them when they arise.

Your project isn't really closed out until you have handed the final output to the sponsors and received their official sign-off. Even then, there is a whole laundry list of things to deal with before you can call it quits on a project. It's called the **closure list.**

The Closure List

Here are the tasks your closure list will include; some of these tasks are described in greater detail throughout the rest of the chapter:

- Completely and fully hand over the final output in its entirety.

- Ensure that the sponsors sign off on final output.

- Set the terms for future project maintenance, if any.

- Complete all final reports.

- Complete all financial reports and processes.

- Complete entire project review.

- Complete employee performance reviews.

- Formally relieve team members.

- Officially close all remaining contracts.

- Dismantle project site or workspace.

- Release any remaining resources.

- Send out project completion announcements via press release or through internal communications.

- Safely store all project documents.

Ending Contracts

One of the first things you'll want to do is to close out any contracts you had that were related to the project's completion. The most important part of this step is to ensure that the terms of each contract are met. You can easily see, at this point, whether the work of each supplier was satisfactory and can take steps to close out the working relationship.

As you close out contracts with suppliers you will formally communicate with them the ending of the project. You'll also want to provide feedback on the quality of the work provided throughout the project. At this point, every aspect of the contract should be completed, to the point that you can formally close things out.

If there are minor items that still need to be finished before you can mark the project successfully completed, you will push those items forward in the priority queue by placing them on what is known as a **punch list**. The project manager and team then work together to complete all of the tasks on the punch list before the project itself be considered completed. The role of the project manager is to begin the contract closure process as the punch list grows smaller, holding onto only the resources necessary to complete the list. When the project manager has deemed each contract acceptably fulfilled, the team can issue a formal written notice to each supplier that officially closes out the contract. The project manager then documents each closure.

The second thing you'll want to do is determine what outputs you are going to hand over to the sponsors and when. This process largely depends on whether the project output has been handed over in pieces throughout its progress or if everything is handed over at the end. It also depends on whether the final output is a straightforward product, a service, or a gradual improvement process. Some handover processes require a gradual transition from the project team to the sponsor.

Before the team actually hands the project over to the sponsor, the project manager usually holds a team meeting to review the project and make sure everything is order to avoid running into any delays on the sponsors' end. This meeting is a good opportunity to ensure that everything on the punch list is complete. Once the team has agreed that everything is ready to go, they can move on to the delivery process.

If the delivery date of the project was clearly defined during planning, you'll want to bend all your efforts toward completing the project on or before that deadline. Sometimes, however, the final delivery date is not clear. In this case, it is best settle on a reasonable completion deadline and try to stick to it. At this point, the team can also agree on how they will celebrate the completion of the project. Planning a celebration can often instill confidence and a high level of motivation among the team members and make for a great ending reward for their hard work..

It is easy to assume that a project is officially closed once the handover process has taken place. However, there are a few more steps to walk through before the completion stage is officially ended. These steps are often referred to **closure tasks.** They make up the details of what must be completed in order to officially end a project. While it may be tempting to rush through these tasks in an effort to be done with the project once and for all, it is important to treat them with as much care as you treated the beginning of your project.

The Official Sign-off

One of the first tasks you'll want to tackle on the closure list is to make sure that the sponsors **formally sign off** on the project to ensure that you've properly delivered everything and that the sponsor will no longer be expecting to hear from you in regards to the current project.

After that, you'll want to see the **final payments** completed to your suppliers. Suppliers can sometimes procrastinate about getting an important details right, so it's a good idea to leave the largest payment for last, as motivation for suppliers to get the work completed. Once a supplier has satisfactorily met all the terms of the contract, the team can sign off and move forward with the final payment.

Time For Review

Next, it's a good idea to schedule a **project review meeting**, which I will go into in more detail when we reach the next chapter. A project review meeting is an opportunity for the team and project manager to get together to review their performance, recount lessons learned, and to identify areas for improvement that came out of the project.

Review Financials

It's important at this point to review all project expenditures to ensure that everything is logged in the final financial statements and that there are no outstanding costs. Then you should review the closure checklist one last time, to ensure that you've completed everything that remained.

Disband The Team

Finally, you'll want to activate the **disbanding stage** of your team by releasing your team members. Unlike contract closure, this step is not considered an official part of the closing process, but it must happen at a distinct point.

Relieving the team means that each person will return to their normal roles within the organization or they will join a new project team. It's a good idea to begin this process toward the end of the project and not wait until the project actually ends. The managers of your team members will need to prepare to get their employees back.

It's also important to remember that the disbanding stage can be emotional for some team members, as it is easy to form relationships within the team and to create good memories. Some project managers find it a great idea to schedule one-on-one reviews with each team member to evaluate their performance and give constructive feedback that they can carry on into future projects. .

Mark The End

The final step in the official closing process is to hold a **closure meeting**. At this meeting, it is customary to review the final outputs with the team, communicate whether any follow-up work will be required, give thanks to the sponsors, shareholders, and team members, and to present a completion report for everyone to sign, as their final official act as part of the project.

Chapter 7: Project Evaluation

The final step of a project is its evaluation period, which occurs after the project is formally and officially closed. It consists of measuring how the project actually went, compared to what was planned. As a result of this comparison, the team can then identify where improvements could have been made. In this way, each team member benefits from the lessons learned and will carry that knowledge on into future projects. In some cases, this evaluation will occur as a prerequisite to project completion.

Project evaluation is fairly straightforward, although the policies and procedures may vary from organization to organization. Depending on the project itself, there are several ways to perform an evaluation, but project managers generally evaluate the extent to which the project objectives were met. This type of evaluation often occurs in a meeting with the project manager, team leaders, shareholders and sponsors.

At other times, an evaluation meeting is set up to allow the team to discuss any lessons learned, receive feedback on their performance, and look for areas of improvement they can pursue as their project management careers Continue.

The Evaluation Report

While informal evaluations may take place during all stages of the project, this one is summarized in the form of a written **evaluation report**. An evaluation report typically includes:

- The projects achieved outcomes.

- The parts of the project that were smooth and successful.

- The parts of the project that were *not* as smooth and successful.

- A summary of the lessons learned.

The evaluation report can also contain other useful information as project managers deem fit. One great piece of information to include is an evaluation of each project stage to see whether the stage went as planned, or whether it veered off track and why. By answering these questions, the entire team can benefit by carrying that information into future projects.

Replicatable?

Another important question the team usually explores is whether they can re-apply in future projects some of the processes they developed for this one. This is an instance where the modularization of project sub-goals can come in handy. There are always processes that are commonly used in many projects; there's no reason these processes can't be standardized for general use in future projects.

Time And Money

Teams commonly perform a final review of the scheduling and budgeting procedures. This usually entails a comparison of the originally proposed budget and its schedule with the actual plan. This is also the opportunity to discuss any events that may have caused the schedule to shift and how effective were the contingency plans that you put in place. It is also an opportunity to review the original time estimates of each contingency plan to determine if they were accurate.

As for the budget, if the actual budget is significantly different from the original estimated budget, the team will determine if the budget estimating method can be adjusted in the future to improve the estimate. .

Risks

After the schedule and budget review, it is common to perform a review of risk mitigation. This is the opportunity to review any estimated risks and compare them to the risks that actually occurred during the project. This is an important time to review risks that occurred but were not predicted, as they probably had the greatest impact on project results. The team will often work together to identify factors or hints that would have led to identifying those risks early on. The team will also work to determine if the response strategies used were sufficient to resolve the issues that arose.

Suppliers

The team will review each supplier contract and discuss the performance of suppliers to decide if they should be added to a qualified list of vendors. In addition to reviewing the suppliers, the team will look at customer satisfaction responses. In the customer satisfaction review, the team will describe their client relationships and determine to what extent the customers should be included in future project decisions.

Customers will have the opportunity to evaluate the team's communication during the project and can suggest ways to improve matters by communicating with a manager of the organization. .

Submitting Reports

Everything discussed in each section of each review will be compiled into two reports to present to the shareholders and to the senior managers of the organization. The shareholder report will essentially be a summary of the project, including a copy of the original goals and how they were met, a summary of the schedule and budget review, and a summary of the customer satisfaction review. This report will be presented subsequently to the customer as another means of communication. The report to managers should include everything reported to the shareholders, but condensed into an executive summary. This will include a brief that covers lessons learned and how they can be applied to future projects. .

Once all of the reports, including scope statements, charters, budgets, contracts, performance reviews, change documents, and signed documents, have been created and distributed to their respective recipients, they should be safely stored where they can be accessed in the future as necessary. The storage of documents will vary by organization; each has its own storage policies. .

Conclusion

If you have decided this field is the perfect career for you, it's time to think about how to fast-track your project management career toward ultimate success. Even if project management is not for you, I hope you will have taken away some strategies and ideas for organizing the projects you take on in your professional and personal life. You can apply the qualities of a great project manager to almost any aspect of your life as a leader, even if you're only "leading" yourself!

As you have discovered, project management is a huge part of any management career. It requires a great deal of knowledge, planning, and attention to detail. You may discover a highly lucrative career if you love a challenge and are ready to put your management skills to the test.

Project management is an art as well as a science. Time-tested strategies and best practices combine with personal wisdom to guide leader and team to effective execution of the project plan.

You now understand how to manage the scope of a project, recruit and manage a small team and most importantly, guide the team with effective communication. You have delved deeply into that most important project stage – planning – and, hopefully, are highly motivated to work through the entire process to finally experience the mouthwatering taste of project success.

You have seen the importance of having a vision along with the drive to carry out that vision, turning it into reality via delegation, inspiration, motivation and communication. Along the way, you have discovered the value of employing specific time management strategies to manage the project effectively from cradle to grave, finishing successfully, on time and within budget.

As a project manager, you now know what it takes to close out a project correctly and completely. With this final skill under your belt, you have all you need to fully develop your inner-project-manager. You also understand how to evaluate the results of your project, for your own growth and for the sake of your team.

The next step is up to you. Are you considering a career in project management? If so, you can begin your search by looking for entry-level project management jobs in your area. They may be as close as the company you currently work for. A LinkedIn account can help. You can use it to meet and talk to experienced project managers. They may be able to provide you with references and connections or even allow you to shadow them as they work on a project.

If you're already involved in project management, your next step is to target a personal area you most want to improve in, then begin implementing the strategies you learned in this book. Are your planning skills weak? Then refer back to Chapter 2 to see what you can do differently. Perhaps you want to strengthen your personal qualities. If so, return to Chapter 4, choose an area to work toward, and implement your own personal self-improvement program.

At the same time, you can use this overview to evaluate your own management skills. Which of the four project stages do you excel in? Which is the most difficult for you? What can you do to strengthen your weak areas and get the most good out of your strengths? What tips can you put to use that will boost your communication skills and your effectiveness with project teams? From the previous chapters, what can you take and apply today to your life?

I wish you the best of luck in pursuing your management dreams!

Thanks for reading. If this book helped you or someone you know, a nice review would be greatly appreciated.

My Other Books

Be sure to check out my author page to learn more about me and see my other books at:

USA:
https://www.amazon.com/author/susanhollister

UK: http://amzn.to/2qiEzA9

Or simply type my name in the search bar: Susan Hollister

Thank You

CPSIA information can be obtained
at www.ICGtesting.com
Printed in the USA
LVHW102008160119
604153LV00013B/213/P